A
BOOKTIFUL
LOVE

I hope you enjoy reading
this collection.

by:

Tolu' A. Akinyemi

~tolutoludo
09/04/2022

Edited by The Roaring Writer Ng.

Typesetting by Word2Kindle

Cover Design by Rewrite Agency

Published by 'The Roaring Lion Newcastle'

ISBN: 978-1-913636-00-5

Email:
tolu@toluakinyemi.com
author@tolutoludo.com

Website:
www.toluakinyemi.com
www.tolutoludo.com

Dedication

To the booktiful ones who built a home in my heart–
Olabisi, Isaac & Abigail Akinyemi. Our love isn't perfect,
or without limitations. But the foundation is booktiful–
thanks for this booktiful love, our booktiful love.

Contents

ALSO, BY Tolu' A. Akinyemi from 'The Roaring Lion Newcastle'

"Dead Lions Don't Roar"
(A collection of Poetic Wisdom for the Discerning Series 1)

"Unravel your Hidden Gems"
(A collection of Inspirational and Motivational Essays)

"Dead Dogs Don't Bark"
(A collection of Poetic Wisdom for the Discerning Series 2)

"Dead Cats Don't Meow"
(A collection of Poetic Wisdom for the Discerning Series 3)

"Never Play Games with the Devil"
(A collection of Poems)

"Inferno of Silence"
(A collection of Short Stories)

Acknowledgements

A big thank you to the editors of the journals below, for giving my poems their first abode.

'Fairytale' first appeared in The Writers Café Magazine.

'Wave', 'Frozen' and 'Defective' first appeared in Wilderness House Literary Review.

A big thank you to God Almighty for crowning me with infinite wisdom to write another book.

To my booktiful partner, Olabisi, thank you for riding through this journey with me. I love you now and always.

A big thank you to my phenomenal children, Isaac and Abigail. I keep learning from you both and I'm super glad to be part of your journey. Always remember that your dreams are valid.

A big hug to my cheerleaders, my ever-supportive parents, Gabriel and Temidayo Akinyemi. Thanks for everything you have done and are still doing.

Special thanks to my editors, Gabrielina Gabriel-Abhiele and Adejuwon Gbalajobi. You both are a breath of fresh air. Thanks for being a part of these booktiful journey with me, I appreciate the fresh insight, and perspective you bring to the table. To my friend Christtie Jay and Mariam Odetoro, depending on which hat you wear, thank you for reading and editing through this body of work in its raw state and challenging me to do better.

To Ridwan Egbeyemi, thanks for the cover art. It's so booktiful!

Huge appreciation to Diane Donovan for a final proofread of this collection. You're highly rated.

To Tayo Sangofadeji, my booktiful creative tribe—you're very much loved on these streets.

A final thanks to everyone who has supported me on this journey that keeps unravelling so many booktiful experiences.

POEMS

One

Isolation

The waves of disruption swept us into isolation.
We stayed home in trepidation behind jarred doors.
Loo rolls became royalty **'highly exalted'** and
the hunt for *sanitisers* left us blue and weary.

Every new day, we grieved the dead.
And every essential shopping trip
was encapsulated with morbid dread. Our lives
hung on a thread like a scene in the land of the dead.

The sight of mass graves
made every breath feel like a prized possession.
We watched the news
and the news fed our hearts, until the gloom

crept from the screens into our souls.
Wreaking havoc so fatal like mortal blows.
Some governments wrapped their arms around
flailing shoulders and protected their vulnerable.

Whilst some others showed their true colours:
Desecrate the commonwealth
whilst the people cling to the strings of survival.
Heroes were born, with some dying in active service.

I will lower the flag at half-staff.
Yes! They were sacrificial lambs on the altar of
   compassion.
In service to humankind.
Conspiracy theories flew on wings

and closet racists went on a rampage.
The crescendo of ignorance was intercontinental.
New words like quarantine, social distancing
and stay home to save lives became our revival song.

After this pandemic halt its blood thirsty reign
of pain and sorrow.
We will learn to live in the way once known,
without the horror of isolation.

We will hold hands in reckless abandon.
We will lock tongues and sway our bodies to new
   music.
We will dream again.
Of a future without the pain of isolation.

Bury Me in a Library

Write my name on a map, when my time is up. Build
    me a statue.
A gigantic statue. Bury me with a catalogue of books.

Don't railroad my chance to walk this hall of fame
with a badge of honour.
You say no smoke without fire.
Lightning kissed dust and we were consumed in a hail
of fire.

Draw me with all my imperfections.
Sketch me with my filth-
with my scars and wrinkles,
mistakes and joy, sorrows and dreams.
Erase nothing, for when I go, I want to go clean.

Write my name in the sands of time
before my sun goes down
and twilight arrives.

Defective

Our banners are held aloft with the inscription
    'Defective'.
We are broken pieces with chests of errors—our
    totality reeks of imperfection.

Our hearts stink like rotten fish. It's dark and hazy in
    there
Like a winter snowstorm causing havoc on the
    runway in Terminal 3.

Call us jigsaw puzzles—
A summation of defects,
defects, and more defects.

It's Okay Not to feel Okay

It's okay not to feel okay,
bruised and battered.
On some days you are shattered
like broken china.

It's okay to be sick and tired,
   feeling blue
 and on a cold streak.

It's okay to feel alone,
abandoned and disgruntled.
It's okay to let go
the baggage of hurt,

   negative wind,
and resentment that have found a home in your heart.
 It's okay to weed out the debris
that wrestles with your freedom.

Frozen

We salivated with the thoughts of greener pastures.
Poverty reached a menopause
and our nights were coloured with wet dreams.

In those dreams, we conjured a future of bliss without
    lack.
Hunger pangs were buried and long forgotten.

Our blazing sun turned dark and our future
became a distant memory.
They sold brown graves for gold-paved streets and
our hapless souls longed for equity.

Thirty-nine helpless humans frozen to death on
account of man's cruelty and lust after vanity.
Ours was a wild goose chase that ended in frozen
    dreams..

Writers

Let's change the world, one writer at a time.
Write those words till the world gets it right.
A writer's haven is a treasure.

Even more—so one with a heart filled with gems.
The human mind is a fertile ground.
Plant seeds with your words and watch it grow.

A writer is immortal, for all seasons.
Don't let anyone gag your voice.
Speak your truth, fearless!

Write for Rights

(For Amnesty International's Write for Rights)

Let's write for the rights of those oppressed—
the voiceless and subdued—
those children in need of warmth from a blanket of
    love.

Cruelty snuggles their bodies like fire.
Write to quench the pain.
Write to save these children from the fate of aborted
    dreams.

Let's write for the vulnerable and defenseless;
words that melt hearts of stone.

Write to change the narrative that history has thrust
    upon us.
Let's write so that we can make it right.

I write to you, Freedom Fighters.
I know your pain—I feel it too.
I know of the gloom that clouds your day.
I know of the bile the status quo serves you for
    breakfast.

But, you are powerful. You can change the world.
Freedom Fighters, let your voices be heard!

Wave

Move
>Unswerving
Like an army of soldier ants.

Breathe with power
>and purpose.
Let out a lungful without shame.

Walk as a Lone Ranger
>In solitude,
If that offers you comfort.

Fly as a power ranger,
break through the enemy ranks
>commando style.

You're the wave,
>The new wave.
Let the world feel the impact of your voice!

Sleep

Sleep is the cousin of death.
So, I charge you to not be carried away.
Kolawole slept till his life faded

and his dreams were obscured.
Sleep is the synonym of dreamland.
Don't spend your whole life sleeping, as you might
end up a dreamer.

Sleep, but don't slip into death
Before you leave the earth.

Your Dreams Are Valid

Your postcode in the newly built expansive house
in the countryside might be invalid.
You are a summation of many things: water bodies,
fire, snowballs, salt and earth.
There are times you look downcast,
At a breaking point, only you didn't break—
You survived just by a whisker.

You asked for a sign. I tell you: the only sign is your
        breath.
The air emitting from your nostrils is enough proof
that your dreams are valid. Dream dreams, dream big,

big dreams. Dream of the ocean making love to the
        sand.
Dream of the "star" who eloped with the *moon*.
Dream those light bulbs into life like Thomas Edison
After failure caressed the inner recesses of his heart.

Dream those dreams of visionary men
who took their failure with a pinch.
Bury those words of fickle men who seek
to dishearten you with heavy words.

Bury your failures.
Dig a grave for your past mistakes
and the voices of perdition.

Your dreams are valid.
Your voice is authentic.
I repeat: your dreams are valid.

Neophyte

It's okay to start small—
Little beginnings
with no endpoint in sight.

It's okay to be tossed to and fro
Like the sand in the ocean.

It's okay to be a blank cheque
Without a signature
and worth.

It's okay to be on the periphery—
Start from rock bottom
Till you reach the zenith.

It's okay not to be okay.
But don't stay too long
With not being okay.

Warrior

I'm not in a competition with you.
We are not opposing athletes on a track.
I'm a man on a journey, rowing my boat
down my life's course.
I'm a warrior,
a giant stallion.

Once despised,
Thanks to the most high,
Now I heave a sigh.

Trial and Error

Life could be a maze of trial
and errors.
We try at every turn
and are submerged in the ocean of errors.

There are days we drown in the pool of mistakes
but we are still here,
animated, peppy
and peripatetic on these paths.

We keep trying even on those nights
we see ourselves overwhelmed, crying.
We make mistakes; we try, we fail,
but we are not deterred by our errors.

Instead, we fail forward.

Cultural

Culture was once the *passport* to showcase your
    identity.
I remember the days when we proudly flaunted our
Native attire with grace and candour.

These days, I see cultural misfits and replicas.
Don't say colonialism. Never mention
those words that might sound politically correct.
Imitate till you irritate those who walked these

glorious paths with grace and charm.
You say it's the new wave. I see cultural misfits,
twisted tongues mashed with fake accents,
lost identities from the curriculum of cultural misfits.

A Date With Hope

Failure only becomes pronounced when
there are gaping holes like broken voices
on a transistor radio. There are days I find myself
on a walk with hope on a lonely street.

Hope took me to new heights.
In those days I was given the boot
and mistaken for the kill. The prey. The noblest
of men became an artifact, a piece of record.

Let's eulogize that man
with a *heart of books*.
He came, he lived,
He was booktiful.

My life has all the colourations of these words.

Life Lessons

Fumble. Stumble, but never crumble.
I didn't start as a winner on Champion's Street, too…
There were days I heard words that rattled
and I crackled.

I thought I would buckle under the weight of failure.
"That was bad" and other depressing words were
      hurled at me,
but I gave no heed—I fought these demons.

Don't say enemies. This wasn't a battle to drop bars
and bottle it all up. Life will bring lessons.
Wear teachability like a bracelet and you will come
out *roaring*.

TWO

Pertinent Questions

The mundane has been glorified by this Twitter
and Instagram generation.
Big Brother Africa's housemates become national
heroes while education takes a back seat.

A first-class degree prize is a pittance.
Short and sweet is the new game.
Make your point in 160 characters.
If it's that important, then it will be worth a read.

Reading walks away in surrender with a look
that screams: "They don't read books anymore!"
On Instagram, it's all a smokescreen.
I see people living in a world of make-believe.

Clout chasers. Slay Queens. Instagram billionaires
with no known source of wealth. The other day,
depression walked in through the back door strutted
the runway of the underachievers and subdued

Till they yearned for freedom.
Stupidity trends for being plain "stupid"
and our headline news is just unworthy:

Star Actor kisses his girlfriend at the mall.
Star Boy eats fresh or stale stew.

Irrelevance is the new cool.
Opinions are now on the cheap,
on sale in that corner shop.

Don't skim through these pertinent questions.
Reflect on them, and don't let them deter you.

Say No to Xenophobia

Mother Africa has been divided into splinters.
The recalcitrant child is from the Southern
    Hemisphere.
Serve them breakfast from the books of history—
They were once living in bondage.

We moved and levelled mountains.
We fought to snatch them from the jaws of apartheid.
Mother Africa has become a laughingstock, by other
    races.
Who will quench this fire from the recalcitrant South?

Ignited on the altar of ignorance,
brick by brick, we give their economy a boost,
but the macabre dance from the south,
watered from the pit of ignorance, will consume
those who fan the embers of xenophobia

to their kin and kindred. Say no to xenophobia
and xenophobic attacks before you're cancelled.

I Belong to Nobody

I belong to nobody, but I'm for everybody.
That was the anthem when we watered our seeds
from the streams of rhetoric.
They coloured our land with false promises

I will bring you heaven on earth. I'll move the River
Niger and Benue and will build a new home for it.
The dollar will bow to the Naira.
You will pluck money on trees

and foreigners will make this place home.
Our blindfolds have been removed. It was all a scam.
He belonged to no other tribe and was blinded
by ethnicity, racial colourations, and prejudice.

He served only one interest.
Can't you see the handwriting on the wall?
He was a brute force of nature/He buried all
        dissenting voices in a canter.

'I belong to nobody' was synonymous
to ethnocentrism, only covered by the veil of deceit.

Aso the Death Post

Aso was supposed to be a rock—immovable and
unshakeable. But it became an altar of tears
and death. Blood flowed freely and ailments
were a stamp-post.Aso became a haunted villa,
caused by the shenanigans of occupants

who dipped hands into filthy places. The spirit of
anguish patrols Aso every hour,
leaving wailing and sorrow in its wake.
Aso needs cleansing from the spirit realm. Let's purge
Aso from the demons of errors and tribalism.

Suspicions and finger-pointing within Aso is rife.
Everyone is a suspect
and the other room gathers dust.
Aso needs spiritual cleansing
and a common-sense revolution.

Erect a Statue for Me in Imo

Erect a statue for me in Imo.
I'm not a deadweight like Zuma
My wardrobe is not littered with Puma shoes.

Build me a statue in Imo.
I'm the son of the soil,
Made in Nigeria like Innoson Motors.

Erect a statue for me in Imo,
The land of zombies & statues.
Dead woods are celebrated in Imo.

The fallen tree and boneless chicken
Both got a golden statue in Imo.
Give me a statue in Imo.

I am a son of the soil.

Twenty Twenty-Three

The star boy is out in the wilderness,
Cast off and discarded.
Those words will make the hard-hearted weep
And say a prayer at the pews.

He was once treasured like a precious ornament.
How dare he trust the arctic,
The home of the kingmakers?

The umpire had barely blown the whistle for the
second round.
They shifted their gaze to the quarters.
Let's sleep walk through this match.

We own twenty twenty-three. It's our shot, it's our
call. We own the land, our cows will vote.
We will unleash even our underage voters
And the treasury is now our regional treasure

For keepsakes and pleasure.
Even this life, we own it.
Call us immortal. We are the hyperborean,
the power brokers of the century.

This throne belongs to us
And our son. The apostle of body bags
Is our anointed for
The throne.

Saints

All the higher-ranking saints in our land
Have been corrupted by the filth of public office.
And the lower-ranking saints
Have been stained and tainted by politics.

Our politics was concocted straight from the pit of
hell. The main motives: Loot the treasury,
let the people starve.

Loot them dry, loot till the grounds become barren.
Loot till They flee by the thousands,
even millions, in search of milk, bucks and Honey.

The skies have been darkened by greed
And our atmosphere is pale.
One quick way of becoming an overnight billionaire
Contingent on the ***deep pockets*** you Lord over:

Stagger into the seat of power. It doesn't matter your
job title-
Photographer, "kitchen cabinet" or "utensil," clothes
hanger or Hangers-on,

A member of the cabal (***call them the
"untouchables"***) or a Jaded pen pusher-
You will keep shouting, "Who is your daddy?"

Cold Room

This is a cold room without *fishes.* Blink twice,
You won't see *bitches o*r the ugly one
who parades our daughters on dog leashes.

This is a cold room for the cold-hearted-
Vile men who adorn scholarly robes
And behave like dogs without flinching.

This is a cold room for loose and depraved men.
Some mount holy pulpits to redeem lost souls
And degrade our Queens.

Welcome to the cold room,
The Altar of sex for marks
And invisible marks and scars.

This is the cold room.
The room where dreams are scarred
And the future is marred.

Strange Dance of Chickens

The chickens are conservative. Some are belaboured
With the orchestra of confusion.
Leave. Remain. Single Market. Confusion. Tyranny.
Backstop. House of Commons. Brexit. Exit. Remain.

ELECTIONS. STALEMATE. ELECTIONS.
Can we just put a full-stop to this anomaly?
This is a strange dance of chickens.
Some are green with envy
And others are liberal to a fault.

It's a campaign of deceit, coloured by lies.
It's a strange dance of chickens
And the chickens are confused by their own wonky
steps.

Ignoramus

I laugh in satire
And choke from the sound of my voice.
A writer lives in the clouds
And draws strength from imagination.

Say tales by moonlight
Or the world of make-believe.
Ignoramus, can't you see?
It was all a joke.

Don't be quick to judge.
It was all fantasy, Fictional.
Don't take this fight personally.
Read with the eyes of the young and insight

Of elders. Read it slow, digest it slowly-
Then we can wave your ignorance off and exit
Ignoramus Street
Without crashing under the weight of the table.

Defunct

You don't have to be dead to be lifeless.
Some are walking dead,
Others are dead men walking.

The head honcho is clueless
And unaware. He is a shadow, a walking shadow.
His answers are incoherent.

"Mister Big, what is your total asset?" He answered
        confidently, "Thirty kine."
The interviewer laughed hysterically, "What is the
        capital of your territory?"
He enthused, with a beam, "*Accra.*"
"What is more important to you, kine or man?"

"Kai, those kine are very important to me.
They are my life/ I can move the world for them," he
regurgitated. His actions beggared belief.
Lifeless is a synonym for the demise of the brightest.

Our Caesar was lifeless.
Never say duplicate,
Body double, or photocopy.
He was just lifeless.

Body Language

Mother's eyes spoke in a gasp of thunder
And a firebolt. There were days she wore looks
that could strike a man dead.

No words/no noise/no telling off,
Just body parts that spoke in different languages.
Mother's tongue was Babel.

There were days she spoke Yoruba, French, Hausa,
English, and Pidgin English, broken, like her spine,
from carrying blues.

Mother's body was the baggage of piercing parts
Swayed by whoever stirs the hornets' nest.
You could be ready for a sting or a truckload of fury.

Revolution Now

(For Omoyele Sowore)

We want a revolution.
We want a revolution now.
Our revolution is sour
Like an unripe mango.

Our democracy took a walk
And found home in 1983.
Our court's judgements are ineffectual.
In the jungle, we handpick sympathetic judgements.

The Chief Justice is a Chief Partner in raping the
system, Bedevilled by ethnic colourations.
Don't ask for a street revolution.
Never mention the word **_revolution_**.

It irks them.
Revolution is an abominable word.
Never say the word revolution
Until there is first an evolution.

The learned SAN can't speak,
the allures of power are an entrapment.
Honesty took a walk to Golgotha.
This isn't democracy.

I see Khaki. Camouflage.
And even more Khaki layered beneath their attires.
Our days of revolution are far-flung.
Give me a silent revolution.

A revolution of the brain, Pen, and imagery
conveyed by intelligence. We want a revolution
now, a silent revolution backed by our best brains
who are tired of the status quo.

Three

A Booktiful Love

Our love was layered in similes and metaphors.
Your love language was erotica,
And meeting you was non-fiction.
I tell you stories coloured in fantasy
And send you off to dreamland with poetry,

Rhymes, and free-flowing verses.
This isn't science fiction or historical fiction.
This was us.
There are days I am buried in the pit of self-help
books.

I read seven ways to be a good husband, and five steps
to show a woman untainted love.
Never say how to be a good wife.
Mute it. Just be silent.

It might lead to horror stories—
A little humour, spiced up with romance,
And our love will be a picture book.
This isn't a mystery or thriller.

It's just me,
A young adult living in fantasy.
I will make you the lead character in my debut novel,
A work of young adult fiction.

I will write out your name in bold in my memoir
And autobiography. Don't say fiction.
This is pure and unadulterated love.
A booktiful love.

Let Him Go

Don't force him to stay if he wants away.
You uttered, *"He promised till death do us part,"*
But the fury in your eyes pulls him to his grave
every hour.

Can't you see the regrets lurking in the corridor of his
    eyes?

The air is stale and his mood pensive.
He draws from the streams of apprehension
And his dilemma is beyond comprehension.
Can't you smell the palpable tension
That floods through the gaping hole on the torn
window net?

The anguish of your words
Are body blows.
End this grief. End this grief called matrimony.
Don't force him to stay if he wants away.

Beauty & Brains

You see broken fragments.
I see flawless beauty,
a gem of monumental proportions.
I colour her in different shades of amazing.

She is bright, a superwoman—
She sets the boardroom on fire with her wisdom.
Her plantation was a harvest of hits.

She was an embodiment of PAIN.
Menstrual Pain. Labour Pain.
And those pains hidden beneath her eyes.

Beneath those pains
Were strength and inner beauty.
She is the definition of *beauty*—
with brains.

Beauty & Priceless

She is beautiful
And priceless.
She is the missing piece in my puzzle—

I won't trade her for a million cowries
Or barter her off to the highest bidder.
I will hypnotize her with a kiss gift-wrapped in love.
I will stand strong and tall with her through all
       seasons.

Our love will brave all weathers,
for her worth is *immeasurable*—
she is my *Prize*.

Beauty & Queening

When you paint her blue
And worship her like a goddess,
She blossoms into rainbows.

When you paint her gold
And etch her name on your veins,
she flourishes like a fountain.

When you colour her with dignity
And saturate her with love,
she blooms into a Queen.

Beauty & Fierce

She is beautiful yet ferocious—
Her emotions are fiery.
She wears despair like a cloth.
Her venom was brutal, like a snake sting.
She was a force of nature.

A victim of her emotions,
She wears despair
Like a well-fitted dress.

At other times
She is a Chameleon,
Sly and deceptive.

She is a captive of her fears.
Her silent tears
And sorrows come in torrents
With her heart damaged beyond repair.

Beauty & Virtuous

She is beautiful
and virtuous,
Realistic
Not materialistic.

She has attributes that were virtues—
Say humility, teachability, and loyalty.
She is made for royalty.
Call her Esther– a king in her Queendom.

She is angelic, gentle,
And a gift to her generation.

Charmazing

Charming and Amazing,
She's a double entendre—
The type that leaves you awestruck and spellbound.
And at other times, gasping for breath.

Her heart is made of gold.
She is a lover /melts hearts,
Even those made of hardwood
And stone.

She is the definition of Jazz,
Not jazz music to serenade your soul.
Hers was undiluted love.
Just Charmazing!

Nostalgia

There are days Nostalgia holds me captive.
I'm a prisoner of my thoughts.
There are memories that bump into me
that spark hysteria.

A country of names and places hang in my throat like
a stillbirth:
Omole /Igbogbo /Ado-Ekiti /Osi-Ekiti /Erin-Ijesha/
Asaba /London /Hertfordshire /Manchester
/Newcastle-Upon-Tyne /Houston, Texas.
Tell me of memories that make you shed tears,

apprise me of those that makes you want to leave your
body behind and run away, voice those memories
that keep you awake in the dead of the night.
Tell me, what makes a man seek shelter away from
home?
How do I wipe clean these memories?
Will my country ever send for me?

Fairytale

The ghost of the bloke I kissed just once near
Poundland pays me a visit in the dead of the night.
My offence: "In ecstasy, I chopped off his lower lip."
He smelt blood and wouldn't let me go. He is desperate

       to have his pound of flesh
in the land of the dead.
    I'm haunted by high heels
and silhouettes of strangers. The other night,

Mother makes a call in her dream, to a strange man.
It might be the same man she has been calling
in her dream for the past seven months. Or one
of the other men who take turns on her creaking bed

before dusk, stealing her virtues until she fades
and becomes dust. I'm haunted by autumn leaves
and the gloom of winter. My life is a fairytale of
imaginary stories and fading memories.

Portrait of a Fake Friend

How do you draw the portrait of a fake friend?
There is no one-size-fits-all approach to label a fake
friend.
Would they be those who hum your closely guarded
secrets to all and sundry?

I do not know what it takes to wear the colour of a
fiendish smile.
A portrait of a backstabber hung precariously in the
home of a once upon a time jolly buddy.

I cannot write one thousand and one metaphors to
label a fake friend.
They could be likened to a grasshopper:
Eat the grass and hop away.

I can tell the smell of a fake friend from a distance:
So awful, like the taste of my mouth after crunching
Bitter Kola.

How do you draw the portrait of a fake friend?
Run when you see their shadow in sight.
As the portrait of a fake friend sends my spirit in
flight.

Lockdown

The shelves are stripped bare, and the spirit of fear
   runs amok.
The vampire of death is dripping in fresh blood.
Shhhhhh! Racists call it the 'Chinese virus.'
This is no hoax or a scene from a horror movie cast in
   Hollywood.

The angel of death has gone berserk! The numbers are
   Frightening.
A strange virus knocked us off our perch.
The World was injected with the spirit of apathy.

The mystical power of loo rolls will be recounted by
   historians.
   Lombardi became a ghost-town,
And the famous French kiss now a distant memory.
The untainted breeze in Times Square sums up the
   chaotic normal.

In every precinct, every day wears its own gloom.
   Some days darker and grimmer.
A raging global pandemic in my lifetime, wears the
   garment of Apocalypse.

Democracy has gone *crazy*!
> Freedom is on lockdown.

The **superheroes** are on the frontline.
A life-saving house arrest and the World on its knees.

They asked for an army of volunteers.
> A community of heroes heeded the clarion call.

> Today, I soaked in the sunshine and its warmth.

I inhaled the air of compassion and fellowship that
abounds.

The news headline reads: Normalcy Returns to
'Wuhan.'
> They can smell the joy of freedom.

With new 'Spring' in my step.
> *I say this too shall pass.*

Grief

How do you grieve the demise of a loved one
with only fading memories to clutch?
How do you fill the gaping hole?
How do you wipe the slate clean?

How do you accept sympathy?
Through Facebook comments and likes. Blurry text
messages with words like *may their soul
rest in perfect peace,* or a register of condolences?

How do you deal with loss?
Does time heal the wounds and we all move on
as if they were never here?
How do you manage grief?

Divorce

There are times you just need to have a break,
Disentangled from the web of a patched-up union.
You can't put square pegs in round holes
no matter how hard you try.

If you can't live in peace, why stay till you're broken
in pieces or it ends in tears?
There are times when we need to face those fears
headlong. Rosemary masked her gloom.

She seemed to be in a perfect Union,
but beneath the make-up was a bruised face and
swollen eye...

In her bank were different currencies of self-deceit
and the belief that tomorrow will bring new rays.
Her joy was far-fetched until she walked away.

Loud Voices

The house with creaking walls shakes from loud
    voices.
How do you end a shouting match?
You pray for silence. Grave silence.

Mother's mouth has a foul stench like the filthy mould
in our garage. Whenever she speaks to Father,
the house heats up. When there is no fire, we choke
from the fumes that pervade the atmosphere.

On some days, the fumes snowball into hails of fire,
burning for days before they reach a ceasefire—
then the cycle repeats in this house where words hit
like missiles.

Grief in Solitude

I know grief.
It tastes like sour omelette for breakfast,
it feels like the cuddled ghost of a stillborn...
Don't dance with me in my grief.

I burn on sunny days,
my mask cracks, and
I tether between intense love and deep hatred.
I rot away in silence.

As autumn leaves lie fallow on the ground, so my skin
        gathers dust.
There are days when I'm yellow. On other days, I'm
        pale with a hint of brown.

Leave me to chew my grief in solitude,
before my life becomes a dusty manuscript.

Starved

My neighbour's marriage hangs on the cross. Sex is the weapon in the hands of his wife, and her silence, whenever he mounts her, makes his head crease in worry. Their nuptial sport is unexciting, unlike what she has with Kemen, her gym instructor, who is a power-tank. There are days she moans in ecstasy while spurting holy waters, clinging unto his strong arms and calling on god while he thrusts her to paradise.

She says to her husband, "Sex is hyped." She would lie on her back like a log, face creased with disgust. "Do whatever you want." The other day I overheard him calling her "Aunty Missionary."

My neighbour is now a nuisance in the neighbourhood. Everyone hides their women from the sex-starved man.

Foundational Mess

"Don't bring an alien to me as a wife.
I won't approve," Queen mother enthused.
I insisted she is the woman of my dreams.
She is the bright sparkle that holds the key to my
	happiness.

The palace, once shining, is now beguiled with visible
	cracks.
The walls gather mould, and cobwebs of rife
between once-cordial royal brothers
hang in disdain at the courtyard.

The gatekeeper says, in a hollow tone,
"Think twice before you say 'I do.'
You can't fix a foundational mess.
You don't have a magic wand. You can't change
	anyone."

A Booktiful Love Story

Love isn't all about vacationing
in the best holiday destinations.
It's not about rose petals
laid on immaculately white sheets in a five-star hotel.

Love isn't flawless, it is imperfect—

Love isn't the coupling of two perfect characters to
form a booktiful love–a booktiful love story.

It could be the bedding of strange bedfellows with
unfamiliar stories. Love isn't all about fat wallets,
for fat wallet can become lean
and the wealthy become paupers.

Love is layered in humane acts. Its foundation is
kindness and humility. Giving without payback,
the right hand is oblivious to the kindness of the left.
That's super love, unconditional love—a booktiful
love story.

Bio

Tolu' Akinyemi is an exceptional talent and out-of-the-box creative thinker; a change management agent and a leader par excellence. Tolu' is a business analyst and financial crime consultant and is a Certified Anti-Money Laundering Specialist (CAMS) with extensive experience working with leading investment banks and consultancy firms. Tolu' is also a personal development and career coach and a prolific writer with more than 10 years' writing experience. He is a mentor to hundreds of young people. He worked as an Associate Mentor in St Mary's School, Cheshunt and as an Inclusion Mentor in Barnwell School, Stevenage in the United Kingdom, helping students raise their aspirations and standards of performance, and helping them cope with transitions from one educational stage to another.

A man whom many refer to as "Mr Vision," he is a trained economist from Ekiti State University (formerly known as University of Ado-Ekiti (UNAD)). He sat his Masters' Degree in Accounting and Financial Management at the University of Hertfordshire, Hatfield, United Kingdom. Tolu' was a student ambassador at the University of Hertfordshire, Hatfield, representing the University in major forums and engaging with young people during various assignments.

Tolu' Akinyemi is a home-grown talent; an alumnus of the Daystar Leadership Academy (DLA). He is passionate about people and wealth creation. He believes intensely that life is about impacting on others. In his words, "To have a secure future, we must be willing to pay the price in order to earn the prize".

Tolu' has headlined, and been featured in, various Poetry Festivals, Open Slam, Poetry Slam, Spoken Word and Open Mic events in and outside the United Kingdom. He also inspires large audiences through spoken word performances. He has appeared as a keynote speaker in major forums and events, and facilitates creative writing master classes to many audiences.

Tolu' Akinyemi was born in Ado-Ekiti, Nigeria and lives in the United Kingdom. Tolu' is an ardent supporter of the Chelsea Football Club in London.

You can connect with Tolu' on his various Social Media Accounts:

Instagram: @ToluToludo
Facebook: facebook.com/toluaakinyemi
Twitter: @ToluAkinyemi

Author's Note

Thank you for the time you have taken to read this book. I hope you enjoyed the poems in it.

If you loved the book and have a minute to spare, I would appreciate a short review on the page or site where you bought it. I greatly appreciate your help in promoting my work. Reviews from readers like you make a huge difference in helping new readers choose the book.

Thank you!
Tolu' Akinyemi

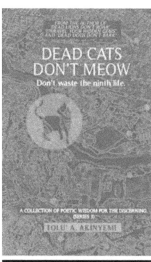

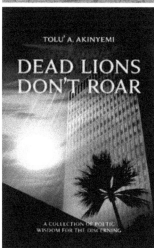

Lightning Source UK Ltd.
Milton Keynes UK
UKHW010703150921
390602UK00002B/95